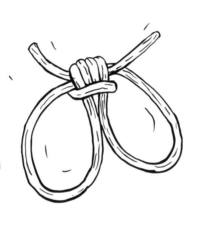

Published by
Princeton Architectural Press
A McEvoy Group company
202 Warren Street, Hudson, NY 12534
Visit our website at www.papress.com

First published in 2017 in Great Britain by Pavilion Books
43 Great Ormond Street, London WC1N 3HZ
Princeton Architectural Press edition first published in 2018
in agreement with Pavilion Books Company Ltd.

ISBN 978-1-61689-718-5

Princeton Architectural Press is a leading publisher in architecture, design,
photography, landscape, and visual culture. We create fine books and stationery
of unsurpassed quality and production values. With more than one thousand
titles published, we find design everywhere and in the most unlikely places.

For Princeton Architectural Press:
Editor: Nina Pick

Special thanks to: Paula Baver, Janet Behning, Abby Bussel, Benjamin English,
Jan Cigliano Hartman, Susan Hershberg, Kristen Hewitt, Lia Hunt, Valerie Kamen,
Jennifer Lippert, Sara McKay, Parker Menzimer, Eliana Miller, Wes Seeley, Rob Shaeffer,
Sara Stemen, Marisa Tesoro, Paul Wagner, and Joseph Weston of Princeton Architectural Press
—Kevin C. Lippert, publisher

Library of Congress Cataloging-in-Publication Data available upon request.

IMPORTANT SAFETY NOTICE

The publishers and the author can accept no legal responsibility for any
consequence arising from the application of information, advice or instructions
given in this publication.

40 KNOTS
AND HOW TO
TIE THEM

Lucy Davidson

Illustrated by Maria Nilsson

PRINCETON ARCHITECTURAL PRESS · NEW YORK

Contents

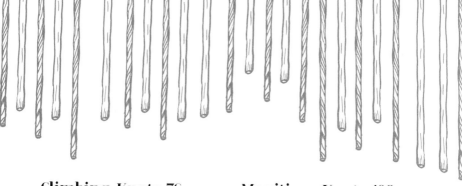

Introduction

One of my earliest memories is practicing tying my shoelaces over and over again. Whether or not my shoes were on the right foot I didn't seem to care; just as long as I got that knot right, I would be happy. I was late a lot, but my laces never, ever came undone. I like to think this was the start of my obsession with knots. Because of growing up in a creative family and serving as a Girl Scout, knots figured quite a lot in my early life.

Knots are diverse and unique. There are thousands of different knots, for all sorts of different purposes, and once you've become acquainted with them, they are easy to use. Knots are an accessible craft, requiring no materials beyond rope. There's something quite magical about taking a length of rope and transforming it into something that you can use or display around the home. Whether it's a practical project like a shopping bag or a purely decorative project such as a plant hanger, a knot can provide a surprisingly versatile solution.

In this book, you will find step-by-step instructions and illustrations on how to tie forty essential knots. The book is divided into four chapters according to each of the four key knot types: classic knots, camping knots, climbing knots, and maritime knots. There are also seven practical and decorative projects you can make using the knots from each chapter. Once you have a basic knowledge, you'll find yourself improvising in no time, surprising yourself with what your imagination can unlock with just a humble knot. Have fun!

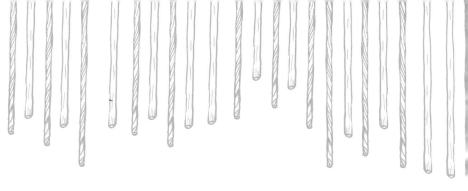

Useful Tips

Start simple. Tying knots comes naturally to some but not so easily to others. Start with the simpler knots in the book and then build your confidence by making one of the projects featuring the knots you have practiced.

Practice, practice, practice. Like learning any new skill, you will have to do it more than once. Tie the knot once and then again, and again, and again. I promise you it will become second nature in no time.

Before cutting any type of rope you should wrap a small amount of tape around it. Using a sharp knife or pair of scissors, cut down the middle of the tape. This ensures that the trimmed ends will not fray.

Have fun with it, practice the knots, and then create the projects as gifts. Your friends will love them, especially as these gifts were made by you. You will then want to carry on making more and more.

Toolbox

The toolbox of a knot enthusiast can contain a variety of contents, ranging from kitchen knives to paper clips, all with their own specific use. Have a look through the most popular tools that might be helpful if you want to try your hand at any of the projects in this book, or if you just want to play around with knots.

Groove Spike

These come in all shapes and sizes, and they are mainly used for separating the strands of the rope. The most common size is around 9 in. (22.5 cm) long.

Scissors

Scissors are pretty self-explanatory and are one of the most useful tools you can have in your toolbox.

Folding Knife

This item is essential for camping trips; if you carefully heat the blade, you can use it to seal your synthetic cords. Please be careful when doing this.

Large Wire Loop
Perfect for those knots where your fingers are too big. Place the metal loop end through the knot, thread the rope through, and pull.

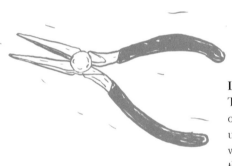

Long-Nose Pliers
These are a great solution for locking onto a piece of cord when you are unable to use your fingers. Most come with a serrated edge that will grip on the rope.

Disposable Lighter
A quick and easy way to seal the ends of your rope so they don't fray.

Sheath Knife
A short knife, similar to a dagger,
is useful for cutting rope and even
lengths of wood.

Tape
Use tape to secure the ends of rope
to stop them from fraying and to help
secure the rope when you try some
of the projects in this book.

Adhesive
White glue, or a stronger adhesive, is
a great material to use to seal the ends
of rope or cord used for the projects in
this book, especially the coaster and
the knotted outdoor mat.

Types of Rope

When it comes to choosing your rope, you will have to consider what you are using it for and its final purpose. It also very much depends on your budget. For the projects in this book you won't need to spend too much, but if you are planning on using the knots for a riskier activity, such as climbing or sailing, make sure to use the highest quality rope you can afford.

Static Kernmantle Rope
This type of rope is constructed with an interior core—the kern—protected by a woven exterior, which is designed to help with strength while adding more flexibility and durability.

Braided Rope
Braided ropes are commonly made from high performance fibers of nylon or polyester. This is an all-around great rope.

Dynamic Kernmantle Rope
This type of rope is specially constructed for and primarily used in rock climbing and mountaineering. This is because the rope has a stretch to it, which makes it a more dynamic rope than the static kernmantle rope.

Laid Rope
Laid rope comprises three sections. The first consists of gathered fibers that are spun into yarns. A collection of these are then twisted together to form strands. The strands are then twisted together to form the lay (direction of twist) of the rope. The twist of the yarn is in the opposite direction to the strands, which in turn is opposite to that of the rope. This creates a counter-twist that holds the final rope together so that it becomes a unified object.

Macramé Craft Cord
This natural rope is easy to work with and is ideal for knotting and macramé projects. It comes in ⅛ in. and ¼ in. widths (3 mm and 6 mm); it is available in different colors and can also be dyed.

Cotton Cord Rope
Another useful craft rope, this braided rope has a width of ¼ in. (5 mm). It is easy to clean and is gentle on the skin.

Terms and Techniques

Knot tying has its own jargon and terminology. I have tried to keep this to a minimum, but here are some useful terms and techniques.

Bight The slack created by folding a piece of rope so that the two parts lie side by side. Please note that a bight is not the same as a loop.

Carabiner A metal link used by climbers.

Crossing turn A loop made when a rope or cord crosses over itself. In an overhand crossing turn, the end is on top; in an underhand crossing turn, the end is underneath.

Frapping The extra turns put on a lashing to make them tighter.

Half hitch A crossing turn made around an object.

Hitch A temporary noose made when a rope is attached to something, for example a hitching post.

Lashing An arrangement of rope used to secure items. Commonly used for connecting poles together, for example when camping.

Loop A partial circle in which the ends of the rope cross over one another.

Round turn A turn in which the rope goes all the way around a ring, pole, or rope.

Slip knot A knot that unties easily when each end is pulled. To make a slip knot, wrap the rope or cord around your hand. Use the tail end to make a loop to pull through the wrap you have made. Pull the loop to tighten the knot.

Splice A technique in which two ropes are joined by untwisting the ends and reweaving the two pieces together.

Standing end The end of the rope that is not being used.

Standing part The section of rope between the standing end and the working part.

Stopper knot A knot that is used to prevent a rope from slipping through a hole or small space.

Working end The end of the rope that is being used.

Working part The part of the rope used in tying a knot.

Safety Information

When working with rope you should always consider your own safety and that of others, so make sure you store the rope carefully and take good care of it. The strength of rope is compromised by a number of different factors, so it is important to be aware of them and take the necessary precautions.

- Even creating the simplest of knots can be hazardous. Please use the best quality rope you can afford— you will find that cheaper rope can leave you with abrasions and splinters that can be painful.

- Try to keep your rope dry; if it gets too wet it can rot and become unsafe and unusable.

- Keep your ropes away from chemicals that could cause rot or weakness. Store them safely, and when transporting them do not allow them to come into contact with any substance that might cause damage.

- Both heat and cold can affect the composition of rope and its safety.

- Keeping your ropes clean can extend their life, especially those that are exposed to salt water. Wash them regularly using detergent or rope cleaner, and dry them somewhere well ventilated, away from direct heat.

- Ideally, always use a wooden post or pole to tie rope from; for safety reasons do not attach it to yourself in case you cause yourself harm.

- Keep ropes tidy, as they can easily be tripped on; coiling ropes is good practice as this stops them from becoming tangled and will keep them from causing harm.

- When creating any of the projects in the book that are designed to hold objects (Wall Hanging, p. 40, Plant Hanger, p. 120) or people (Hammock, p. 136), make sure the item is thoroughly tested before use.

Caution: Tying knots with rope, as well as partaking in sports associated with this practice, can be dangerous and inherently includes the risk of serious injury and damage—especially when incorrectly handled, gripped, or tied. Carefully review each knot or project, and ensure you thoroughly understand the use of all tools, materials, and applications before use.

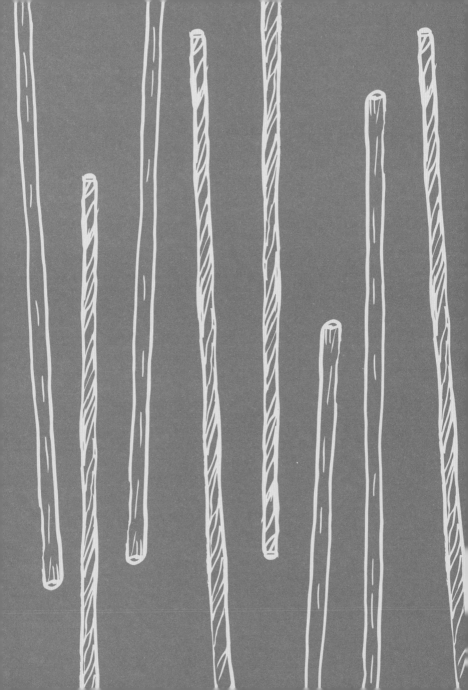

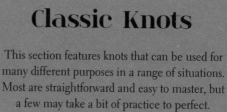

Classic Knots

This section features knots that can be used for many different purposes in a range of situations. Most are straightforward and easy to master, but a few may take a bit of practice to perfect.

01

Thumb Knot

The Thumb Knot, also known as the Overhand Knot, is one of the most rudimentary knots and forms the basis of many others. It should be used if the knot is intended to be permanent and is often used to prevent the end of a rope from unraveling or from passing through a block. The Thumb Knot can be tied in two ways, crossing over or under, but for some knots this can cause many mistakes. Make sure you check which way to knot if using this technique when trying out the other knots in this book.

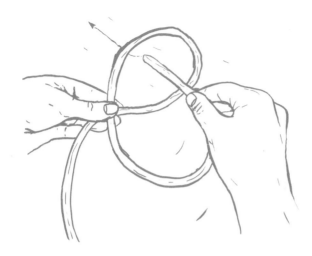

1. Take the rope and create a loop. You can do this by wrapping the rope around your thumb—this is called a crossing turn. Pass one end of the rope through the loop.

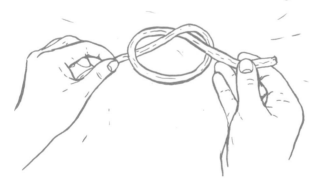

2. Pull both ends away from each other to tighten the knot. While tightening, slide it into place.

02

Blood Knot

The Blood Knot, also known as the Double Overhand Knot, is simply a logical extension of the regular Thumb Knot but made with one additional pass. The result is slightly larger and more difficult to untie.

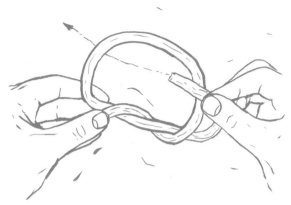

1. Take the rope and create a loop. You can do this by wrapping the rope around your thumb—this is called a crossing turn. Pass the end of the rope through the loop twice.

2. Pull both ends of the rope to tighten the knot.

03

Reef Knot

The Reef Knot, sometimes known as a Square Knot, is a simple binding knot. It is usually used to secure a rope around an object, or most commonly, to tie shoelaces. It is also one of the many knots used in macramé. You can practice this knot in the Wall Hanging project (see p. 40).

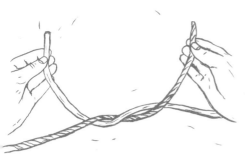

1. Take two pieces of rope, and with one piece in each hand, cross one piece over the other. Take the end of the bottom rope and cross it over the top rope; repeat by bringing the bottom rope across the top again.

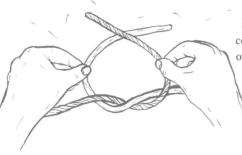

2. Bringing the two ends that have come out on top, cross the right cord over the left cord and pass it through the loop.

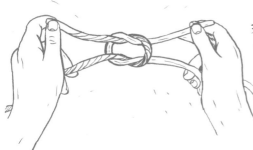

3. Bring the ends of each rope together, and pull both pairs apart to tighten the knot.

04

Reef Bow

The Reef Bow is also used for tying shoelaces and for bow ties. There are several ways of tying the Reef Bow. This knot can be extremely useful as it has the stability of the Reef Knot, but it is a lot easier to untie. Simply pull the ends away from the center of the knot! The loops are sometimes referred to as "rabbit ears," especially when teaching the knot to children.

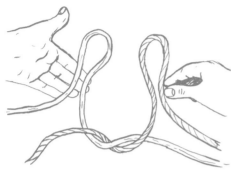

1. Take two pieces of rope, and with one piece in each hand, cross one piece over the other. Take the end of the bottom rope and cross it over the top rope; repeat by bringing the bottom rope across the top again, making sure your working ends are much longer. Double the working ends, creating a loop in each hand.

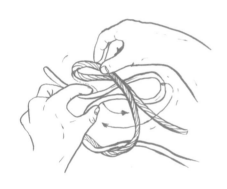

2. With the doubled rope, bring the two ends that have come out on top, cross the right cord over the second cord, and pass it through the loop.

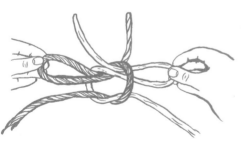

3. Pull the doubled ends to tighten the knot. If the short working ends are pulled before you tighten, it will slip and come undone.

05

Hunter's Bend

This knot is commonly used for joining two ropes together. It consists of interlocking Thumb Knots and is a very simple knot to tie. It is thought that this knot was invented in the late 1970s, but other people believe it has to be much older considering how simple it is. One use for the Hunter's Bend is in knitting; it is an excellent knot for joining the ends of your yarn together— the last thing you want is for your garment to unravel.

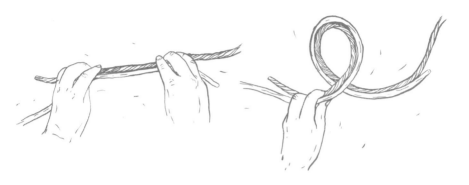

1. Lay two pieces of rope next to one another with the working ends facing in opposite directions.

2. Keeping the ropes together, make a loop. Make sure they lie the same way as shown in the diagram.

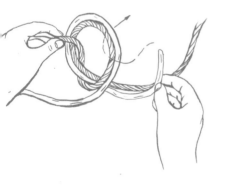

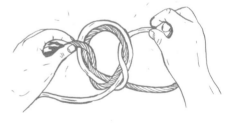

3. Take the bottom cord end and bring it first up and then down through the loop. Carefully lead the other cord end under both cords and bring it up through the loop.

4. Tighten the knot by pulling the cord ends in opposite directions.

06

Bowline

This is one of the most useful knots you can learn. It has many applications but is commonly used for forming a fixed loop, large or small, at the end of a line. This knot is extremely useful for climbing, as even after tension is applied, it is easy to untie. Because of this, it shouldn't be trusted in extreme situations.

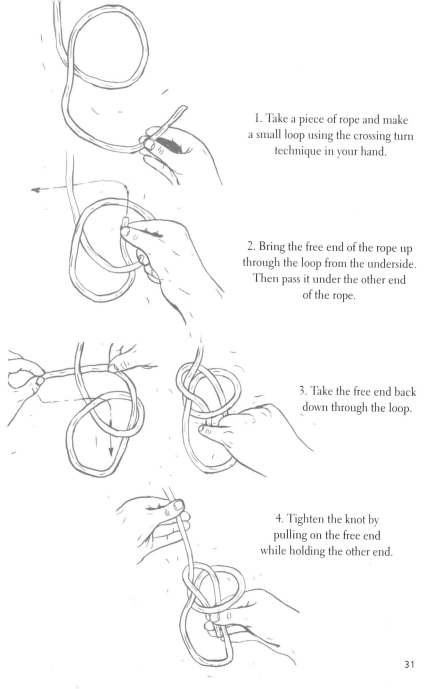

1. Take a piece of rope and make a small loop using the crossing turn technique in your hand.

2. Bring the free end of the rope up through the loop from the underside. Then pass it under the other end of the rope.

3. Take the free end back down through the loop.

4. Tighten the knot by pulling on the free end while holding the other end.

07

Monkey's Fist

The origin of the Monkey's Fist was for use on sailing ships, but these days it is used more commonly as a decorative knot. It can be made in any size, depending on the thickness of the rope and how many turns you make. This knot may take several attempts through trial and error to get a perfectly round and tight-fitting knot! You can always insert a plastic ball to firm up the center when the knot is being used for decorative purposes.

1. Take your rope and wrap it around your hand three times as shown in the diagram. Poke the end through the gap between the middle and ring fingers.

2. Loosen the rope and pass the working end around the coils. Repeat twice to complete the three turns. Pull tight.

3. Gently remove your fingers from the knot.

4. Make another three turns where your fingers used to be, perpendicular to the previous coils.

5. Pull tight and then, working back to the start, gently tighten and arrange the coils so they are neat.

6. To tighten the first three coils, reverse the order to tighten and complete the knot.

08

Cat's Paw

This is a common hook hitch for slings; it is usually tied
in the middle of a sling with the load hanging beneath it.
The knot will undo instantly when removed from the hook.
This is the hitch that is always used for heavy loads.

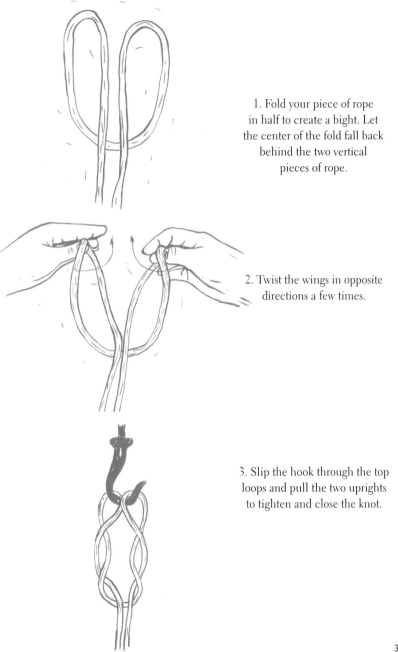

1. Fold your piece of rope in half to create a bight. Let the center of the fold fall back behind the two vertical pieces of rope.

2. Twist the wings in opposite directions a few times.

3. Slip the hook through the top loops and pull the two uprights to tighten and close the knot.

09

Tom Fool's Knot

This knot forms the basis for a number of decorative
and functional knots. It can be used in sailing and camping,
and for general use.

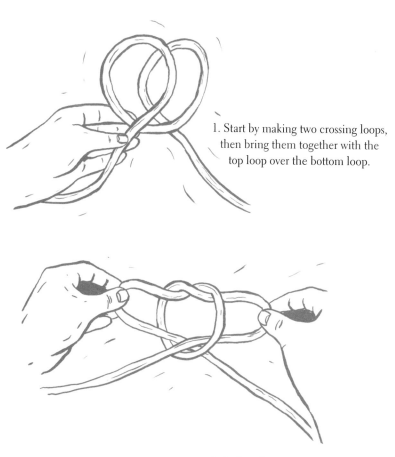

1. Start by making two crossing loops, then bring them together with the top loop over the bottom loop.

2. Pull each inner half loop through the outer side of the opposite loop. Pull until tight.

10

True Lover's Knot

Also known as the Fisherman's Knot or Englishman's Knot, this type dates back to the mid-1400s. Its most common use is for joining the ends of a fishing line because it is so simple to tie. It is also a decorative knot, and it symbolizes—as the name suggests—true love, with the two intertwined Thumb Knots (see p. 20) locking together.

1. Lay two pieces of rope next to one another with the working ends facing in opposite directions.

2. Tie a Thumb Knot (see p. 20) at one end, making sure you tie it around the other cord. Repeat with the other end.

3. Carefully tighten both knots and pull the two standing parts (see p. 16) of the rope. This will automatically move the two Thumb Knots toward one another.

4. The finished knot should look like the main illustration (see p. 38 opposite).

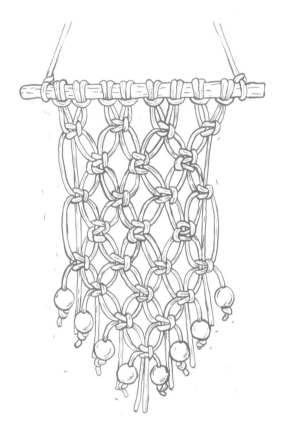

Wall Hanging

If you're looking to decorate the house or refresh a certain space, why not start with the walls? You can create this wall hanging using one simple knot, the Reef Knot (see p. 24). The beaded decoration is optional.

You Will Need

– *1 piece of dowel measuring 12 in. (30 cm)*

– *8 lengths of cord measuring 80 in. (2 m)*

– *8 wooden beads (optional)*

– *1 length of thinner cord measuring 20 in. (50 cm)*

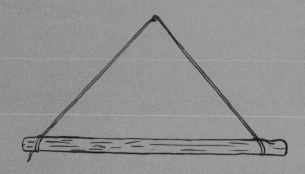

1. Tie the thinner cord around both ends of the dowel, and hang from the wall or a door handle.

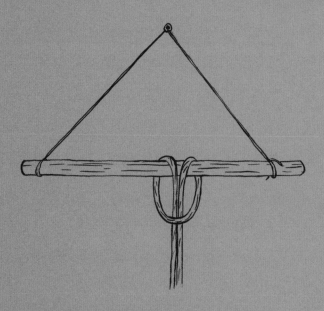

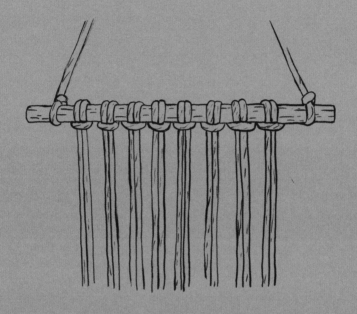

3. Repeat with the rest of your working cords. The cords should hang side by side and be evenly spaced along the rod.

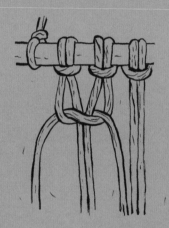 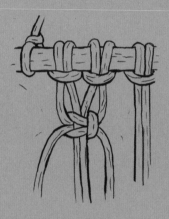

4. Take the first two sections and, using the outer cords, tie a Reef Knot (see p. 24) around the middle cords.

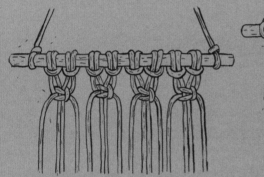

5. Working in pairs, repeat Step 4 along the dowel so you are left with four evenly spaced Reef Knots.

6. For the second row, tie three Reef Knots, leaving out the first and last two cords.

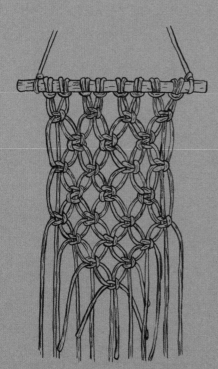

7. Repeat this pattern for four more rows. You will notice that you start to run out of rope. To create the tapered end, decrease the number of knots on each side for two more rows.

8. Starting with the outer cords and leaving the middle two cords free, thread a bead onto every other cord and secure with a Thumb Knot (see p. 20); this is optional.

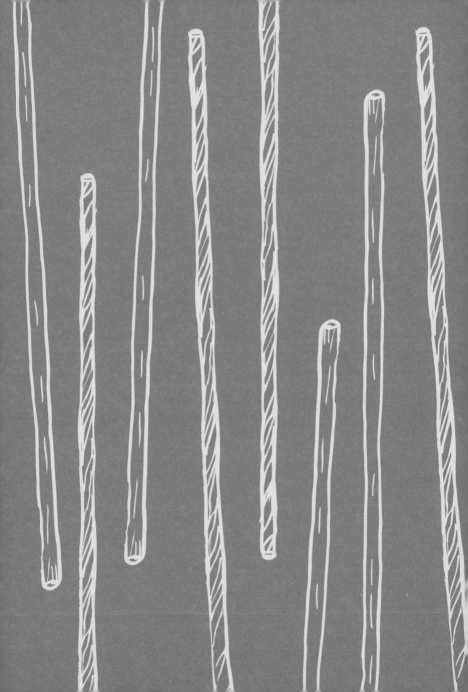

Camping Knots

These days camping is not quite the "back to basics" experience it used to be, but there are invariably occasions where knots are required to tie equipment together, secure your gear to your car roof, or even create something to sit or lie on. Here is a range of useful knots that can help with all those tasks and more.

11

Slipped Figure of Eight

This knot is very strong and can be used to hitch a hammock or a large piece of cloth. It is easy to slide this knot into place—for example, around a tree—and it can be easily released by pulling on the tail.

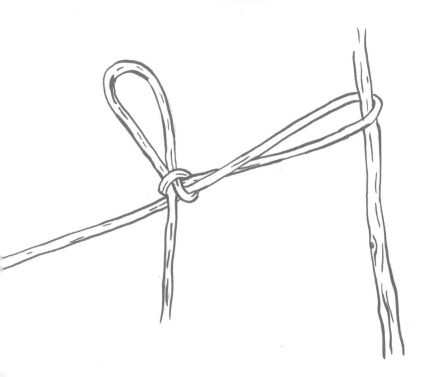

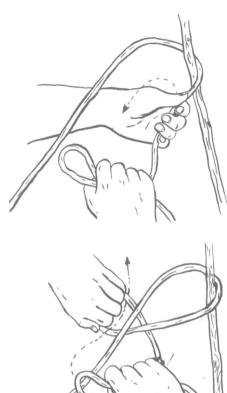

1. Pass your rope around a pole as high as you can reach. In your right hand create a bight. Reach under the rope with your left hand and pull. As you pull the rope with your left hand, twist it down to make a loop.

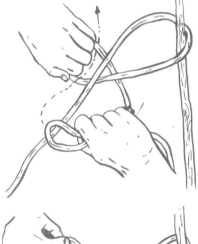

2. With your right hand, place the bight over the rope and through the loop in your left hand.

3. Pull the loop through and tighten the knot. The weight of your load will tighten the knot, but if you are making a hammock, you should also tension the rope with an additional knot at the other end.

12

Sheepshank

The Sheepshank has several features that allow a rope to be
shortened. It can also be a very attractive knot. The knot will
remain secure under tension but can fall apart easily when this
tension is removed. It is great for those times camping when you
need to shorten your guide ropes.

1. Place the rope into an S-shape and make a loop in the rope just below the left bend. Bring the top bight through the smaller loop below.

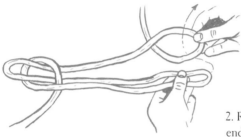

2. Repeat this process on the opposite end, bringing the right bight through the smaller loop you have made at the top.

3. Pull the ends tight to secure the knot.

13

Pile Hitch

The Pile Hitch is a knot used for attaching rope to a pole or other structure and is also extremely quick to tie. It can be tied in the bight without access to either end of the rope, making it a valuable tool in most situations.

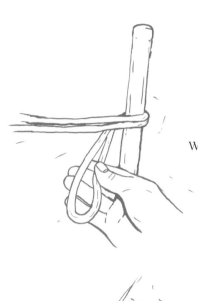

1. Loop your rope to form a bight. Wrap it around a post or other upright object from front to back.

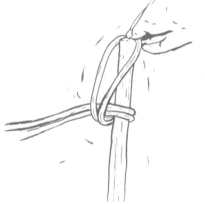

2. Cross over the standing parts of the rope and slide the open end of the loop over the top of the post.

3. Pull the rope tight.

14

Tent Pole Hitch

The Tent Pole Hitch ensures that you don't lose slippery
or unruly objects, as this knot keeps those items in place —
perfect for when you need to carry those tent poles!

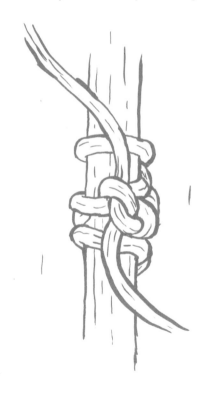

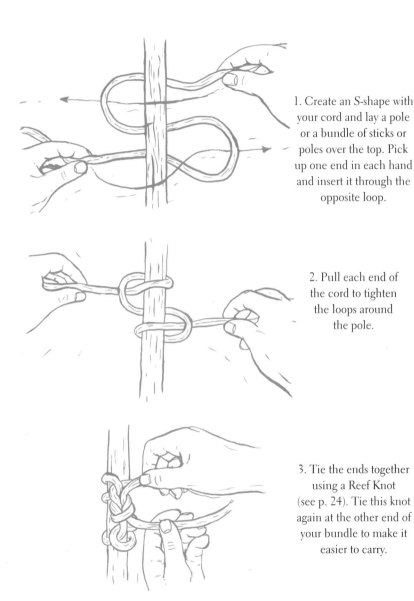

1. Create an S-shape with your cord and lay a pole or a bundle of sticks or poles over the top. Pick up one end in each hand and insert it through the opposite loop.

2. Pull each end of the cord to tighten the loops around the pole.

3. Tie the ends together using a Reef Knot (see p. 24). Tie this knot again at the other end of your bundle to make it easier to carry.

15

Rope Ladder Knot

Be prepared to use a lot of rope when making this particular knot! It uses a few of the techniques from the other knots we have already covered, and it is best made using stiff rope. If you have enough rope, you could use this knot to make an entire ladder.

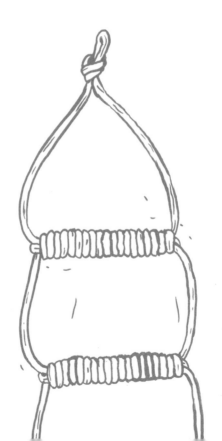

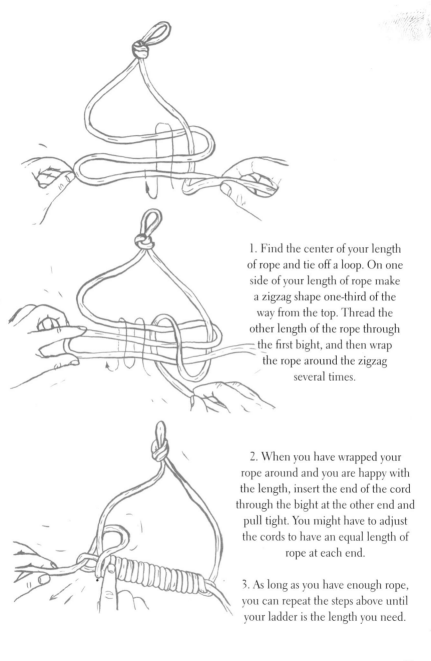

1. Find the center of your length of rope and tie off a loop. On one side of your length of rope make a zigzag shape one-third of the way from the top. Thread the other length of the rope through the first bight, and then wrap the rope around the zigzag several times.

2. When you have wrapped your rope around and you are happy with the length, insert the end of the cord through the bight at the other end and pull tight. You might have to adjust the cords to have an equal length of rope at each end.

3. As long as you have enough rope, you can repeat the steps above until your ladder is the length you need.

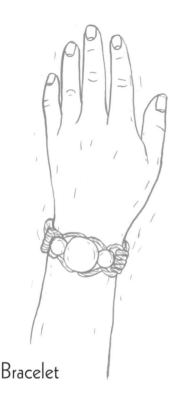

Bracelet

This is a perfect craft activity for a rainy night in the tent. The Rope Ladder Knot (see p. 56) is simple and quick to learn, and it looks great as a bracelet, either with or without the beads.

You Will Need

– *1 length of cord measuring 60 in. (1.5 m)*

– *1 small bead to close the bracelet*

– *1 large bead (optional)*

– *2 smaller beads (optional)*

1. Take your piece of cord and fold it in half to create a loop in the middle. Tie a Thumb Knot (see p. 20) ¼ in. (1 cm) from the end of the loop.

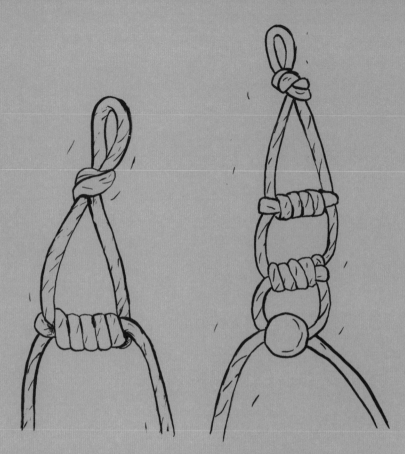

2. Tie a Rope Ladder Knot (see p. 56) ¾ in. (2 cm) from the Thumb Knot. Make sure both sides are the same length, otherwise the bracelet will hang unevenly.

3. Tie another Rope Ladder Knot ¾ in. (2 cm) from the previous one. You can either carry on just using Rope Ladder Knots or you can add some beads for decoration.

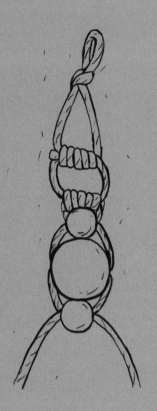

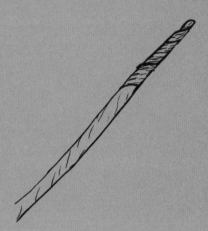

4. Attach the beads by threading the rope on the left of the bead though the hole toward the right, and the rope on the right of the bead through the hole in the opposite direction.

Tip:
Wrap a piece of masking tape around the ends of your cord to make it easier to thread the beads.

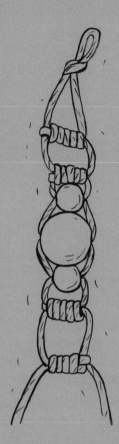

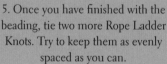

5. Once you have finished with the beading, tie two more Rope Ladder Knots. Try to keep them as evenly spaced as you can.

6. To add the bead for the clasp, tie a Thumb Knot about ¾ in. (2 cm) from your last knot. Thread both of the cords through the bead and then secure with another Thumb Knot. This bead will fit through the loop at the other end of the bracelet to secure around your wrist.

16

Icicle Hitch

The Icicle Hitch is a great knot for tying around a post when you want to lift it or pull it along. This hitch will stay in place when holding a substantial load and even grips a tapered post—hence the name "Icicle" Hitch.

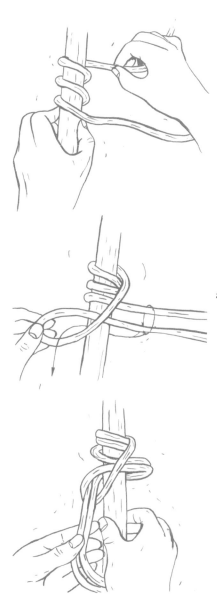

1. Wrap the rope around the pole three times.

2. Drape the working end down and across the turns on the pole, and then twist to make a loop. Take the two ends back around the pole, and then poke through the loop.

3. Pull the two ends carefully to tighten the knot.

17

Asher's Bottle Sling

This particular knot is commonly used to attach to a bottle
(as the name suggests) and is easily tied to your camping rope
or to yourself. It is very easy to remember and is therefore
very popular.

1. Tie the ends of your rope together to create a closed loop using a Reef Knot (see p. 24).

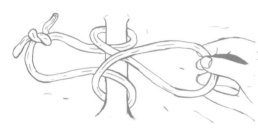

2. Twist the unknotted side of your rope, and wrap your looped cord around the neck of the bottle, bringing the sides of the loop up and around the neck so one loop passes through the other.

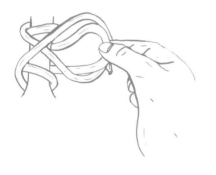

3. Take the other end, wrap it around the neck, and pull up through the loop. Pull tight to create the sling.

18

Trucker's Dolly Knot

This hitch knot is commonly used for securing loads on vehicles, such as trucks and wagons. This general arrangement, with loops and turns, has been used for centuries. The knot is quite secure and can be easily undone once unhooked. It is also good for securing items to your roof rack or trailer—for example, all the extra baggage you need when you go camping.

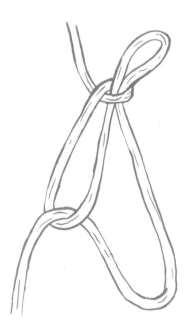

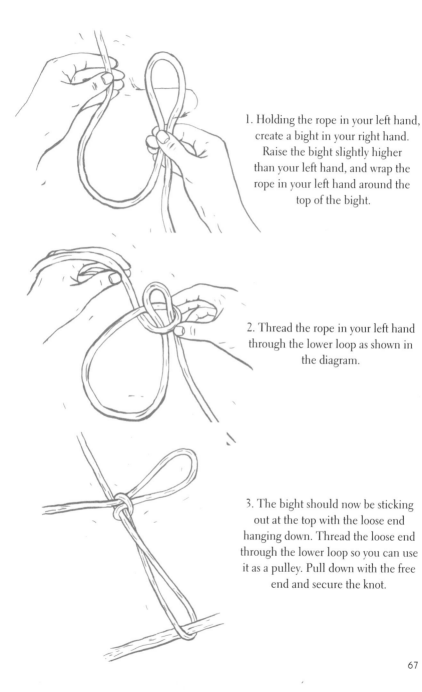

1. Holding the rope in your left hand, create a bight in your right hand. Raise the bight slightly higher than your left hand, and wrap the rope in your left hand around the top of the bight.

2. Thread the rope in your left hand through the lower loop as shown in the diagram.

3. The bight should now be sticking out at the top with the loose end hanging down. Thread the loose end through the lower loop so you can use it as a pulley. Pull down with the free end and secure the knot.

19

Crown Knot

The Crown Knot is one that can be tied at the end of your rope when you notice the ends are fraying. It will end up being double the diameter of the main rope, so it's no good if you need to thread it through a tight space.

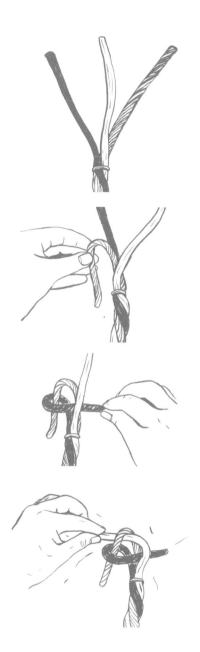

1. Take one end of your rope and tie a Constrictor Knot 3 in. (7.5 cm) from the top. Start by tying a Clove Hitch (see Step 1, p. 71), and then take the end over and then under the first turn of the Clove Hitch before tightening.

2. Split the rope into three, unraveling until you meet the Constrictor Knot. Wrap a small piece of tape around the ends of the three cords that have been created.

3. Separate out the ends; take one of them and fold it in half between the other two.

4. Wrap the next cord around the looped cord and thread between the loop and the third cord.

5. Fold the third cord over the second cord and through the loop created by the first cord. Each cord should now be held down by another; tease all three sections and tighten.

20

Square Lashing

This is a perfect camping knot, especially if your tent poles let you down. You can easily bind two poles together, and it is designed to bear the load of scaffolding! The uses for this knot are endless: you can make support frames when there are two trees close together; you can support a table with a pair of poles or branches lashed together; and you can also construct a fence by hammering some poles into the ground and attaching bars using Square Lashing.

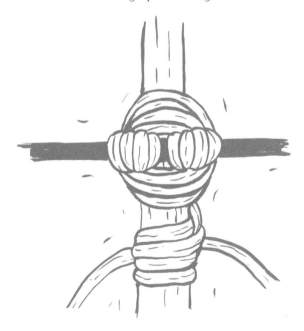

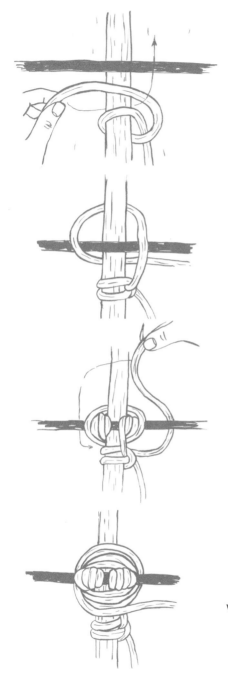

1. Tie the rope to the vertical pole using a Clove Hitch (shown here) and pull it tight. Place the second bar on top of the vertical pole just above the Clove Hitch.

2. Take the rope up and over the top pole, then around the back of the vertical pole. Bring it down over the top pole and then behind the vertical pole again. Pull tight.

3. Repeat Step 2, taking the rope around the pole three times and pulling it tight each time.

4. Next start the frapping turns that will tighten the original turns even more by bringing the rope under the turns and between the two poles. Wrap the rope around three times and secure with another clove hitch.

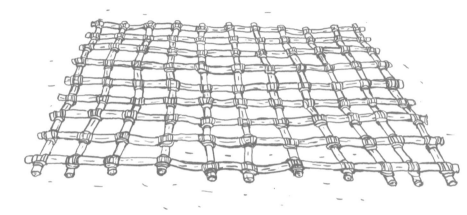

Knotted Outdoor Mat

This is a great addition to any tent—perfect for muddy boots. You could also use this technique to make a place mat or a trivet to use in the kitchen.

You Will Need

– *9 lengths of thick cord or rope measuring 32 in. (80 cm)*

– *11 lengths of thick cord or rope measuring 16 in. (40 cm)*

– *99 lengths of thin cord or string measuring 16 in. (40 cm)*

– *Scissors*

– *White glue*

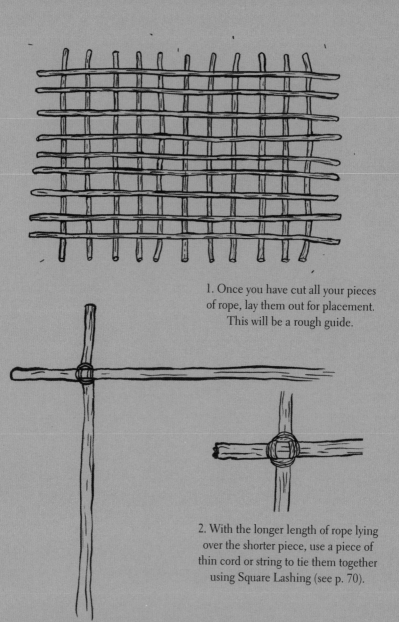

1. Once you have cut all your pieces of rope, lay them out for placement. This will be a rough guide.

2. With the longer length of rope lying over the shorter piece, use a piece of thin cord or string to tie them together using Square Lashing (see p. 70).

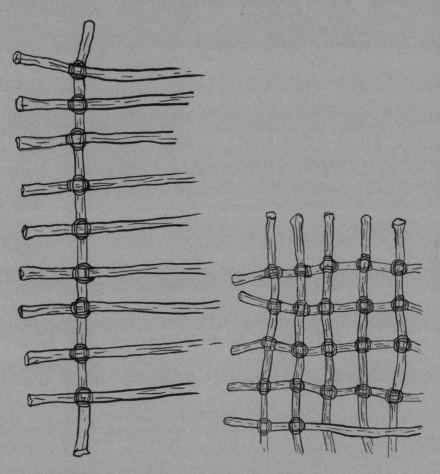

3. Work down all nine rows, repeating your Square Lashing.

4. Continue all the way across; you will start to see your mat taking shape.

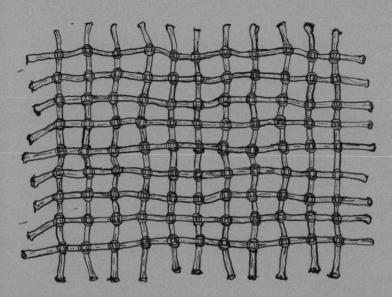

5. Once complete, lay the mat flat; if it seems bumpy, use some books to weigh the rope down and leave overnight.

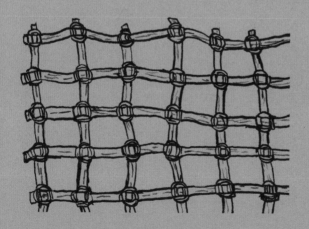

6. Trim all the ends and secure them by dabbing them with white glue.

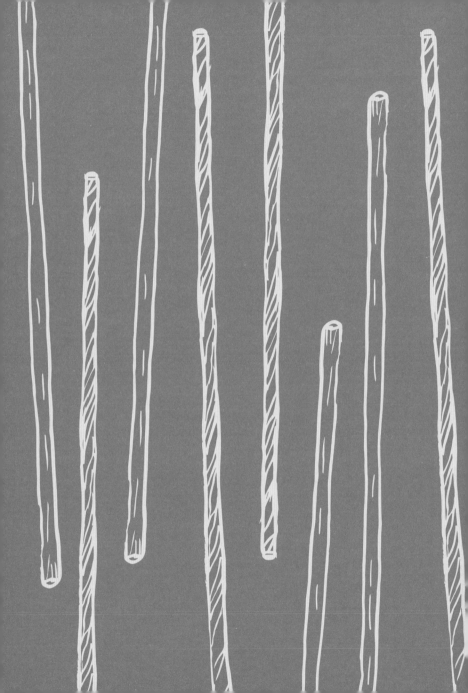

Climbing Knots

This section contains some of the best-known climbing knots. While it is fun to learn how to tie them, they should only be used for climbing after extensive training. Bear in mind that the knots you tie will not only determine your own safety but also that of fellow climbers.

21

Munter Hitch

The Munter or Italian Hitch is an important knot for climbers. It works best with large-shaped carabiners and should only be used with a locking carabiner. Pay extra attention when tying this knot as it can cause kinks and twists in the rope.

1. Pass the rope through your carabiner and create a loop.

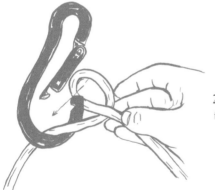

2. Open the carabiner, and thread the loop over the hook. Close the carabiner gate and tighten.

22

Water Knot

Also known as the Ring Bend, climbers usually use this knot for joining webbing tape to create slings. These can then be used to loop into their carabiners. This knot is extremely strong and flexible, perfect for joining ribbon together or mending shoelaces.

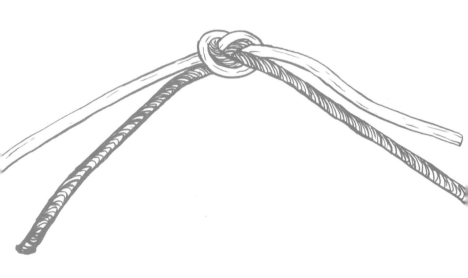

1. Tie a Thumb Knot (see p. 20) in one end of your tape, cord, or rope. Make sure the tape lies flat while making this knot.

2. Feed your other tape end through the knot. You will be creating a second Thumb Knot. Once you have successfully fed the other tape through, work the knot closed and pull tight.

Coaster

This is a very simple knot to master, and the same technique can be used to make larger mats using extra lengths of rope. You can even make matching placemats too!

You Will Need

- *2 lengths of cord measuring 40 in. (1 m)*
- *A disposable lighter*
- *Pile of books or heavy weight*
- *White glue (optional)*

1. Start by tying a Water Knot (see p. 80), leaving about 4 in. (10 cm) at one end. Keep the knot quite loose and lay the ropes next to one another so they stay flat.

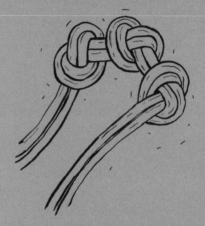

2. Tie another Water Knot, keeping this knot close to the first. Again, make sure the knot is as flat as possible by keeping the ropes together and not twisting them.

3. Continue tying Water Knots around in a circle.

4. Complete the circle of knots. Roughly five knots work well for a coaster.

5. Push the ends from the last knot through the first knot to complete the circle. Push the ends from the first knot through the last knot to finish.

6. Trim the ends close to the knots and burn carefully with the lighter to prevent any fraying; take care not to burn any other parts of the rope.

7. You can also secure the knots using a little white glue to stop any movement, but this is optional. Once dry use a pile of books or a heavy weight to flatten the knots so your cup won't wobble.

23

French Bowline

This knot is also known as a Portuguese Bowline. It is similar
to a standard bowline but uses several loops so there is less
likelihood of damage occurring to the object you have secured
your rope to. It can be used during a rescue when climbing: the
victim can sit in one loop and the rescuer can adjust the other
loop around her own body.

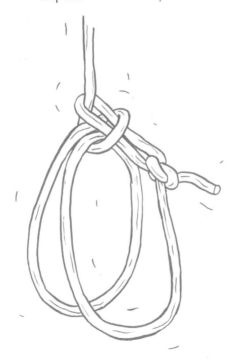

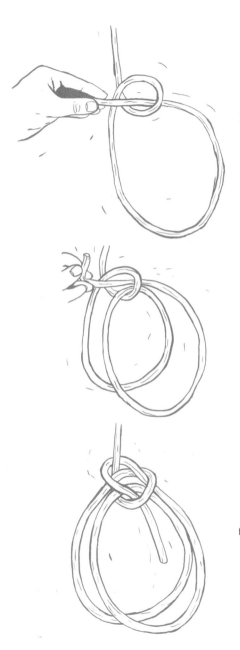

1. Start by making a small loop in your rope. Form a second, larger loop with the other end of the rope and pass the end through the small loop.

2. Make another large loop, and once again take the end through the small loop.

3. Take the end of the rope around the back of the main line, and thread through the eye. Pull through and tighten. Finish the end off with a Thumb Knot (see p. 20).

87

24

Alpine Butterfly Knot

The Alpine Butterfly Knot, or simply the Butterfly Knot, forms secure loops in the middle of a rope. Mountain climbers tie the Alpine Butterfly in the middle of their ropes, where it can be used to attach a hook or a carabiner. It can take a load in any of the three directions, independently or together.

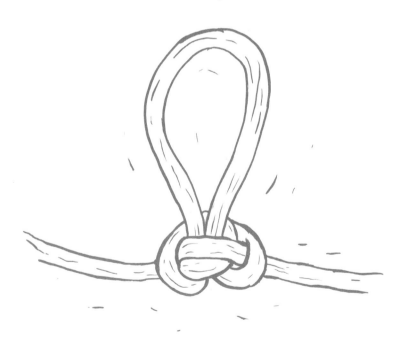

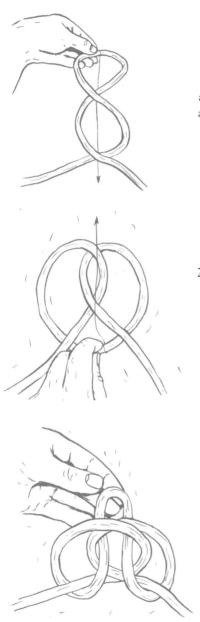

1. Fold your rope in half to create a bight, and twist clockwise to form a figure of eight. Fold the top of the bight back behind the twist.

2. Bring the bight back up from the bottom and through the crossing between the two loops.

3. Pull all three ends to tighten the knot.

25

Spanish Bowline

The Spanish Bowline is a double loop knot that can be used to lift a person: placing a loop around each leg, you can then hold onto the vertical part of the rope. This knot has a very elegant symmetry to it, and once you have mastered the technique, it can be tied very quickly.

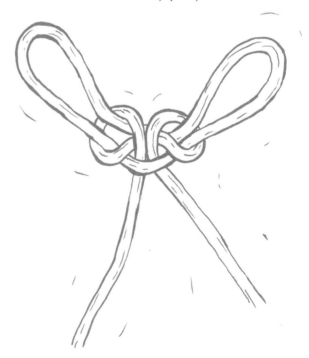

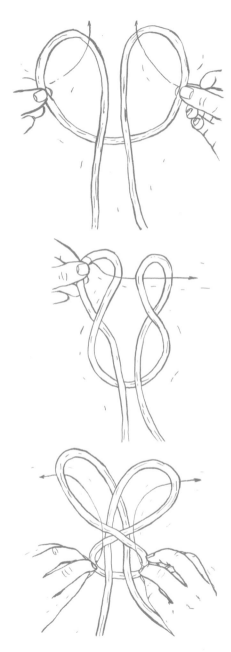

1. Take a long piece of rope and fold it in half to make a bight, and allow the bend to drop behind; this will create a loop on each side. Twist each loop toward the middle.

2. You should now have two figure eight shapes. Pass the top left loop through the top right loop.

3. Bring the two sides of the lower loop up through the two bights above. Gently tease into place and pull tight.

26

Prusik Knot

You can use the Prusik Knot to secure a loop to a line that is already tight. The knot will slide when it is not weighted but will jam solidly once loaded. Mountaineers can use this knot to form footholds to help them climb a vertical rope up a mountain. Ideally the loop needs to be made in rope or cord that is almost half the thickness of the main rope you are working with.

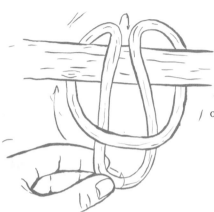

1. Tie the two ends of the rope together to create a large loop. Pass one end of the loop behind and over your main rope, and then pass it through the other end of the loop.

2. Pass the loop back around the main rope, and then through the loop again. Pull tight.

27

Prusik Handcuffs

These are a temporary measure and should only be used for recreation and not actually for restraint. The handcuffs can easily come undone.

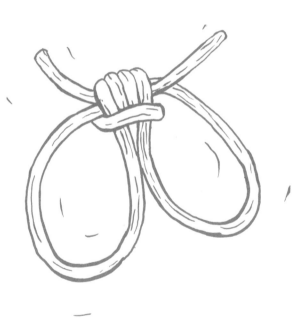

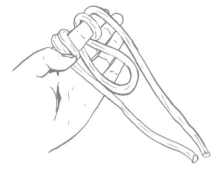

1. Use the same method as for the Prusik Knot (see p. 92), but this time tie the knot onto your finger instead of onto a main rope. Create a large loop, this time leaving the two ends of the rope at the front. Pass the loop behind and over your finger, and then back to the front. Repeat, bringing the loop through to the front again.

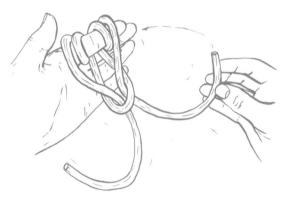

2. Pass one end through the loop on your finger and pull through. Repeat with the other end in the opposite direction.

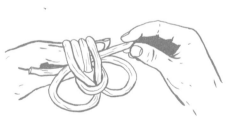

3. Take the knot off your fingers, pull the slack out of the coils, and the handcuffs will be ready to use.

28

One-Handed Bowline

The bowline can be easily tied around the waist with one hand. This knot can be used in any emergency situation that requires you to hold onto a rock with one hand, leaving only one hand free. Hopefully you will never need to use this knot for this purpose, but do take the time to learn it just in case.

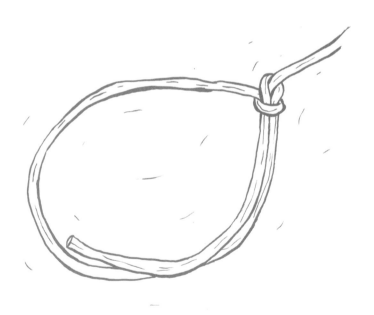

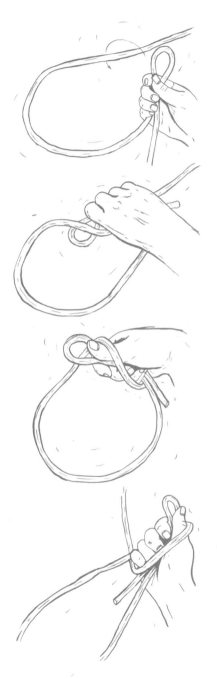

1. With the hand that you will be using to tie your knot, grasp the rope, make a small bight, and clench your fist. Then take the bight over the main rope.

2. As you take your hand across the rope, the back of your hand should be facing upward.

3. Twist your hand down and toward your body and then away again.

4. At the end of the twist, the loop that you just created should run across your knuckles.

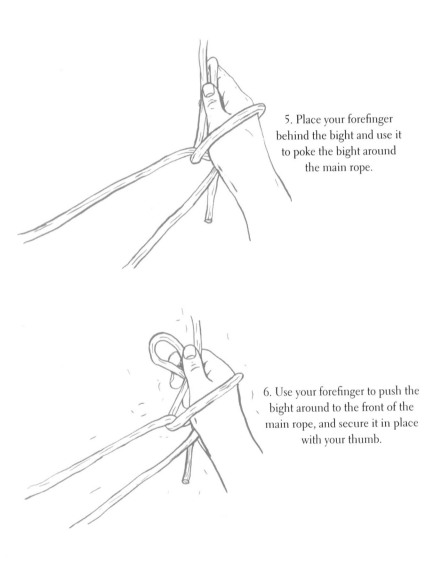

5. Place your forefinger behind the bight and use it to poke the bight around the main rope.

6. Use your forefinger to push the bight around to the front of the main rope, and secure it in place with your thumb.

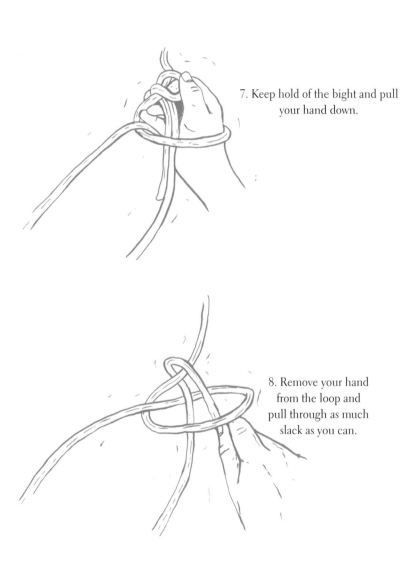

7. Keep hold of the bight and pull your hand down.

8. Remove your hand from the loop and pull through as much slack as you can.

29

Tarbuck Knot

This knot was developed for use by climbers, and was initially used with stranded nylon ropes. It is now advised that this knot not be used with kernmantle rope as it can damage the outer covering of the rope (sheath). This knot is useful when a rope is subjected to heavy or sudden loads, as it will slide to a limited extent, thus reducing shock.

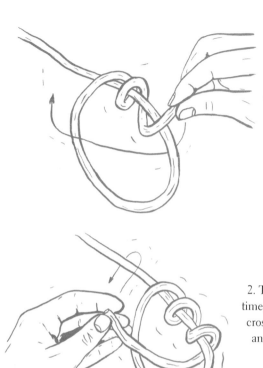

1. Create a loop and wrap the end of the rope around twice, working into the loop.

2. Take the rope around a third time, bring it out of the loop, and cross in front. Then take it over and around the vertical rope.

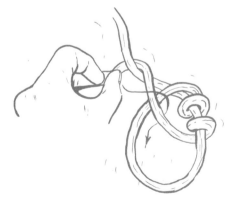

3. Bring the rope back to the front and feed it down through the last loop created. Pull tight.

30

Bachmann Knot

The Bachmann Knot is a friction hitch popular with climbers, and it can be tied using a round cross-section carabiner. It is sometimes used when the Prusik Knot (see p. 92) becomes stuck and the climber is unable to move it along the rope. The Bachmann Knot is tied by hooking the Prusik loop through the carabiner and wrapping it around the rope several times, leaving the rope through the carabiner.

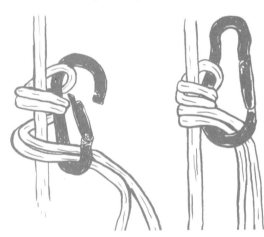

1. Hold the carabiner against the vertical rope. Hook your loop of rope around the carabiner. Wrap both ends of the loop around the vertical rope, and then pass them through the carabiner. Repeat once more.

2. Pull down on the ends of the loop of rope to tighten the knot around the vertical rope and carabiner.

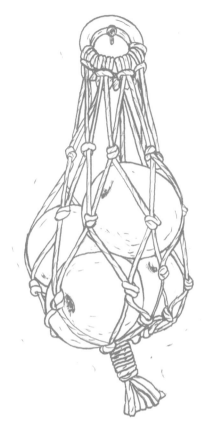

Knotted Bag

A perfect little project to carry all the essentials, you can make this bag as large or as small as you like. The only knots you will need to know are the simple Prusik Knot (see p. 92) and the most basic knot, the Thumb Knot (see p. 20).

You Will Need

– *8 lengths of cord measuring 40 in. (1 m)*

– *2 wooden or metal rings/handles*

– *1 length of cord measuring 20 in. (50 cm)*

1. Take one of your long cords and fold it in half. Tie a Prusik Knot (see p. 92) around one of the wooden handles.

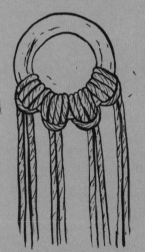

2. Repeat Step 1 until you have tied four cords onto each wooden handle.

3. Putting your two handles together, tie the outermost pieces of rope together 3 in. (7.5 cm) from the top. Tie them together using a Thumb Knot (see p. 20).

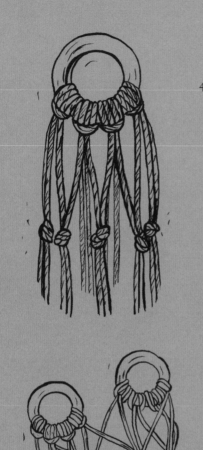

4. Continue to tie cords together in adjacent pairs.

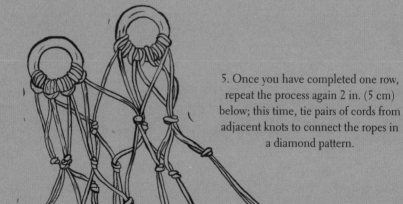

5. Once you have completed one row, repeat the process again 2 in. (5 cm) below; this time, tie pairs of cords from adjacent knots to connect the ropes in a diamond pattern.

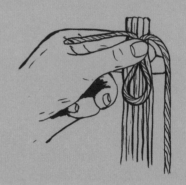

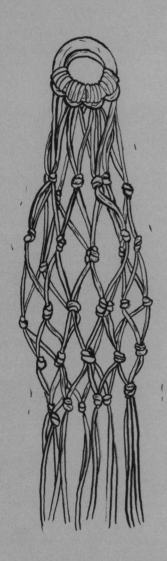

7. Once you reach the end, bind the cords together using the 20 in. (50 cm) piece of cord and form a loop, leaving 2 in. (5 cm) of rope at the top.

6. Continue with the rows of Thumb Knots until you come to the end of your cords.

8. With this cord in your right hand, wrap it tightly around the other cords—about ten turns should be enough.

10. Pull the upper tail tight.

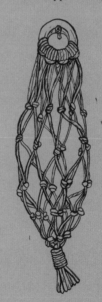

9. Thread the tail of the cord through the loop at the bottom.

11. Trim the ends at the bottom of the bag.

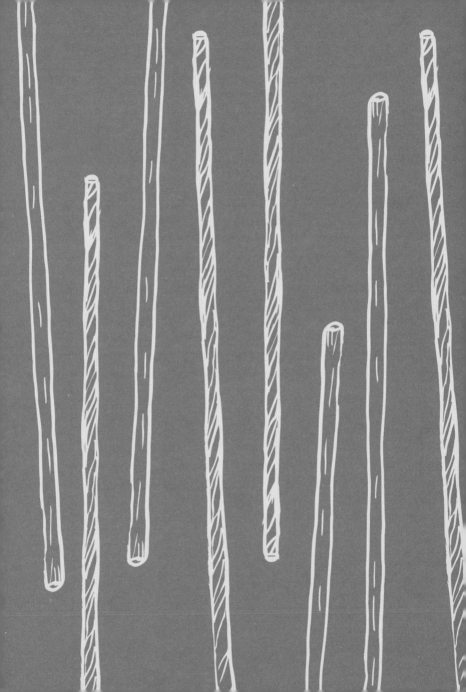

Maritime Knots

Knots are widely used in both fishing and sailing. This section includes some of the most useful for each activity. Many sailing knots have been around for centuries and have changed little over time. Fishing knots use many of the techniques that have already appeared in earlier sections but employ thinner lines and are on a smaller scale.

31

Anchor Bend

The Anchor Bend is the knot generally used to fasten a line to an anchor. It is perfect for securing boats, as the knot becomes tighter and thereby more secure when the rope gets wet and slippery. This is a useful knot to know when on the water.

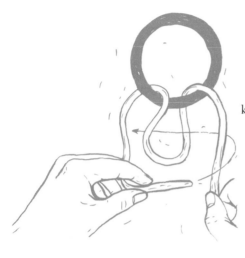

1. Take your rope and wrap it around the ring, as shown in the diagram, making sure that you are keeping the rope quite loose. To make the first half hitch, feed the rope through the loop that is hanging down, and pull.

2. To form the second half of the hitch, loop over the vertical rope and back through, and then tighten.

32

Carrick Bend

This knot joins two ropes together and also forms the center of the very decorative Josephine Knot; practice this while making the plant hanger (see p. 120). It is a traditional knot that is simplest when used with thick heavy rope. For a mat-like appearance the knot may be adjusted so that it is looser and the ends can emerge on the same side.

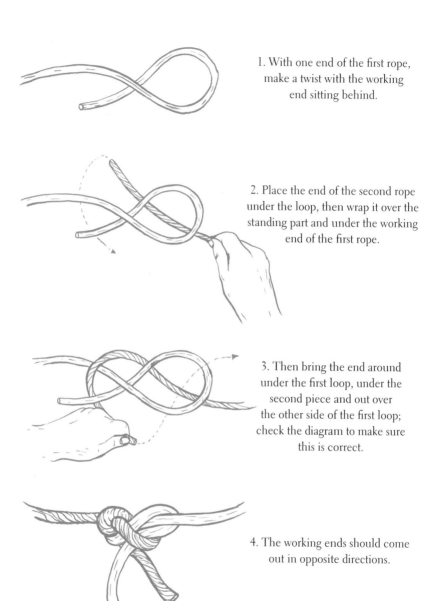

1. With one end of the first rope, make a twist with the working end sitting behind.

2. Place the end of the second rope under the loop, then wrap it over the standing part and under the working end of the first rope.

3. Then bring the end around under the first loop, under the second piece and out over the other side of the first loop; check the diagram to make sure this is correct.

4. The working ends should come out in opposite directions.

33

Boom Hitch

Often referred to as the Decorative Hitch, this knot requires a single tuck and a Thumb Knot (see p. 20) and the result is a neat, attractive knot. It is one of the simplest knots to tie, as each turn just wraps on top of the previous turn. However, it should be tightened carefully because on both sides it is possible to disturb the sequence of the wraps and make a mistake.

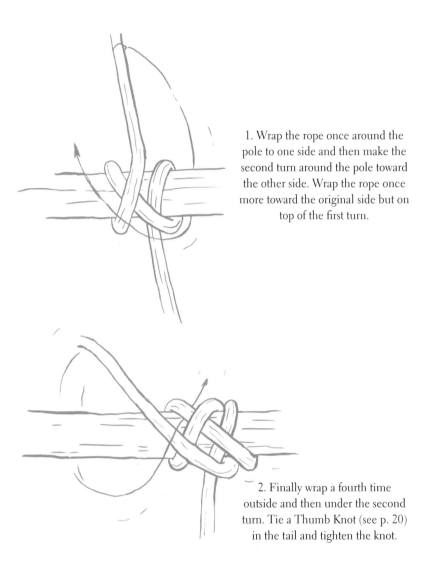

1. Wrap the rope once around the pole to one side and then make the second turn around the pole toward the other side. Wrap the rope once more toward the original side but on top of the first turn.

2. Finally wrap a fourth time outside and then under the second turn. Tie a Thumb Knot (see p. 20) in the tail and tighten the knot.

34

Mooring Hitch

This is a temporary knot that can be released quickly with
a pull on the free end. It can be tied tightly to another vessel
or mooring, and at any point along the length of the rope,
so you can reach and release it without getting out of your boat.

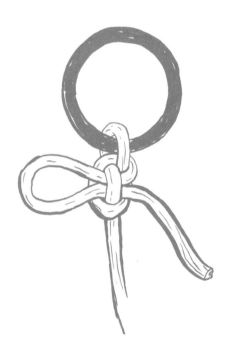

1. Pass the rope through the ring and form a loop with the free end, making sure the free end sits behind the rope. Make a bight in the standing rope and pull it through the loop.

2. Create a bight in the free end; pass it over the crossing loop and through the bight in the standing rope. Pull to lock the rope into place.

35

Turk's Head Knot

This is perfect as a decorative knot, especially with two or three passes. The main advantage of this knot is that it can be expanded into larger, beautiful knots. The number of bights is the number of loops it will have, creating the decorative edges.

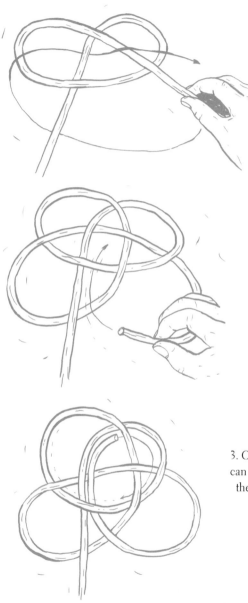

1. Make a loop with the working end. Make a second loop on the left on top of the first. To form the third loop, weave the working end under and over twice, as shown by the arrow in the diagram.

2. Make the fourth loop by weaving the working end over and under once more as shown.

3. One turn is now complete. You can carry on following the path of the first turn until you have the desired number of turns.

Plant Hanger

This plant hanger is a great way to hang your plants, flowers, and succulents. The only knots you need to master are the Josephine Knot, which is a simple configuration of the Carrick Bend (see p. 112), and the Reef Knot (see p. 24).

You Will Need

– 1 wooden ring

– 8 lengths of cord measuring 80 in. (2 m)

– 2 lengths of thinner cord measuring 20 in. (50 cm)

– Plant pot or vase

– Flowers or plant

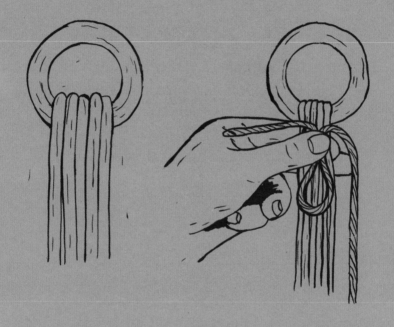

1. Hang your wooden ring on a hook or a door handle. Thread all eight lengths of cord through the wooden ring. This will leave you with sixteen working cords.

2. To secure your cords to your wooden ring, take one piece of the thinner cord and form a bight as shown.

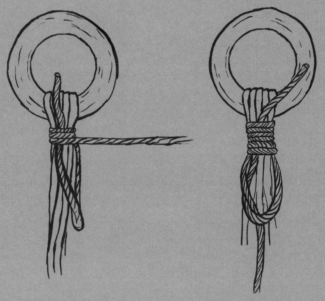

3. With the working end of the thin cord in your right hand, wrap it tightly around the sixteen cords—six turns should be enough.

4. Pass the end of the cord through the loop at the bottom.

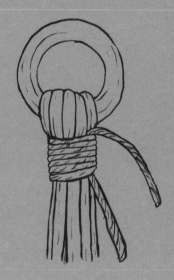

5. Pull the upper tail tight.

6. Pull until the loop is tucked halfway inside the wrapped cord. Trim your ends.

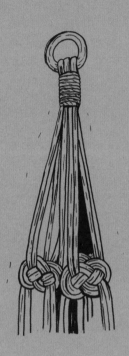

7. Take four of the hanging cords and, leaving a gap, tie a Josephine Knot. A Josephine Knot is a decorative version of the Carrick Bend (see p. 112). Make sure both standing ends enter from one side and both working ends exit from the other.

8. Turn your ring around and work on the next four cords, repeating Step 7. You will end with four separate knots.

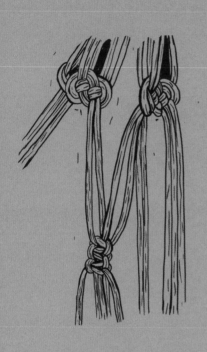

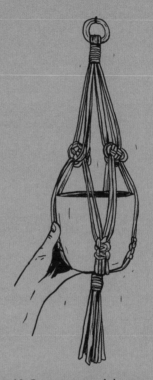

9. Leaving another gap, tie two Reef Knots (see p. 24) using four cords.

10. Secure your ends by repeating Steps 2–6 and trim the ends. Place a plant pot or vase into the hanger, adjusting the knots as you go, and it's finished!

36

Albright Knot

This is a versatile knot that can be applied to small lines when fishing. It has a wide range of uses and is moderately easy to tie. It is commonly used to join the fly line to the backing line, but it can be used whenever you want to join two fishing lines together.

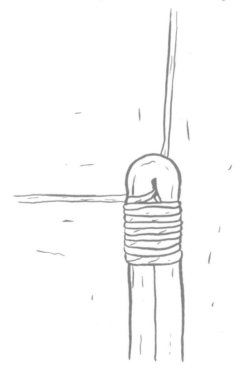

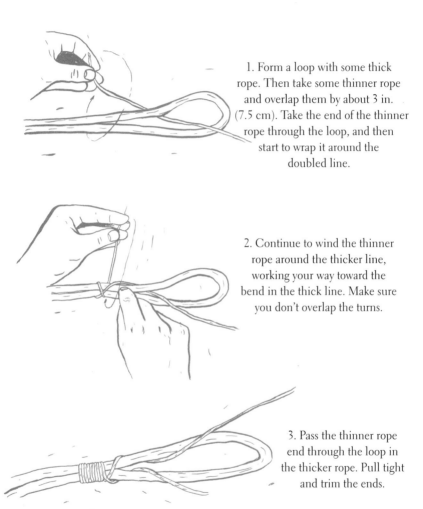

1. Form a loop with some thick rope. Then take some thinner rope and overlap them by about 3 in. (7.5 cm). Take the end of the thinner rope through the loop, and then start to wrap it around the doubled line.

2. Continue to wind the thinner rope around the thicker line, working your way toward the bend in the thick line. Make sure you don't overlap the turns.

3. Pass the thinner rope end through the loop in the thicker rope. Pull tight and trim the ends.

37

Nail Knot

The Nail Knot is a popular knot that has stood the test of time. It also works with a small hollow tube instead of a nail, and so it is sometimes called a Tube Knot, depending on what you are using. If you do use a nail, the nail will be removed and the rope fed through the hole.

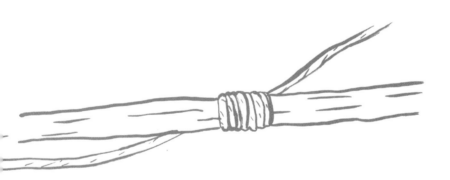

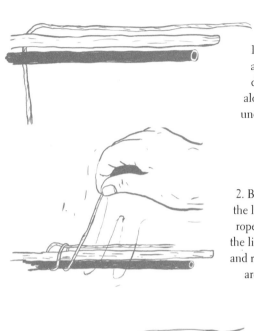

1. Using a nail or a tube, lay it against a rope as shown in the diagram. Place a piece of line alongside them and take the end under both the rope and the tube.

2. Begin to wrap the working end of the line around all three pieces—the rope, the tube, and the other end of the line. Keep the turns close together and remember to not overlap. Wrap it around approximately six times.

3. Once you reach the end, insert the working end of the line through the tube.

4. Pull the tube free from the loops; the rope will be slack, so tighten carefully, and then trim the ends.

38

Netting Knot

This is the traditional knot used in most netting for fishing and traps. It is useful to know if you are sailing and need to catch your own supper! Once you have mastered this knot you can create your netting by repeating these steps using a continuous piece of rope. The Netting Knot can also be used to create your own hammock (see p. 136) or bag.

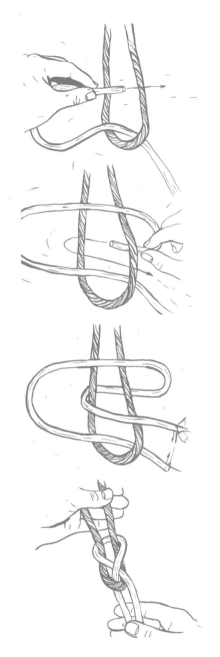

1. To create the most common Netting Knot, which is the Sheet Bend, make a bight in your rope. Thread another piece of rope through the bight from behind, then make a small bight and wrap the end around the main bight.

2. Bring the end through the smaller bight you have just created.

3. Hold the two ends of the working rope together in one hand.

4. Holding both ends of the other rope in your other hand, pull both ends of the working rope downward to tighten the knot.

39

Dry Fly Knot

The Dry Fly Knot is probably one of the best choices for connecting flies to your line. It is a strong knot and can be used in wet or dry conditions.

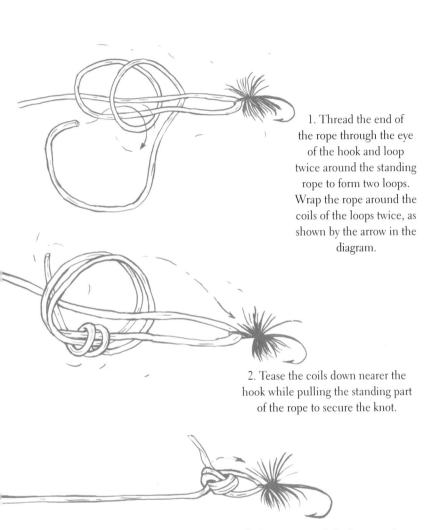

1. Thread the end of the rope through the eye of the hook and loop twice around the standing rope to form two loops. Wrap the rope around the coils of the loops twice, as shown by the arrow in the diagram.

2. Tease the coils down nearer the hook while pulling the standing part of the rope to secure the knot.

3. Continue until the knot touches the hook, and then trim the end.

40

Perfection Loop

The Perfection Loop, which dates back to the 1600s, is the easiest way to make a small loop in the end of your fishing line. It would most commonly be found at the end of a fly line.

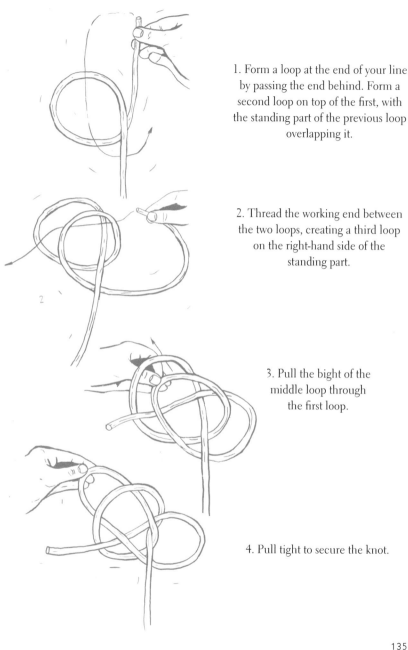

1. Form a loop at the end of your line by passing the end behind. Form a second loop on top of the first, with the standing part of the previous loop overlapping it.

2. Thread the working end between the two loops, creating a third loop on the right-hand side of the standing part.

3. Pull the bight of the middle loop through the first loop.

4. Pull tight to secure the knot.

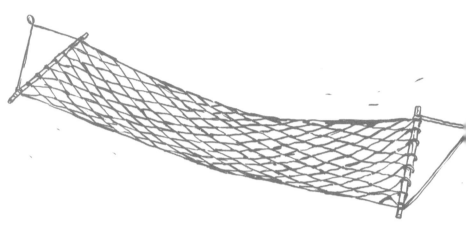

Hammock

Who doesn't love lying back and
relaxing in a hammock on a warm
summer's day? As this project mainly
uses just one knot—the Netting Knot
(see p. 130)—you'll be enjoying the
fruits of your labor in no time!
This project uses a huge amount of
rope, and the easiest way to work with
this much is to roll it up into a ball or
wrap it around a wooden shuttle.

You Will Need

– *2 pieces of dowel measuring 40 in.
 (1 m) wide*

– *Roughly 755 ft. (230 m) of laid
 rope depending on the length of the
 hammock; this should be enough to
 make an average-size hammock*

– *2 lengths of cord measuring
 60 in. (1.5 m)*

– *Masking tape*

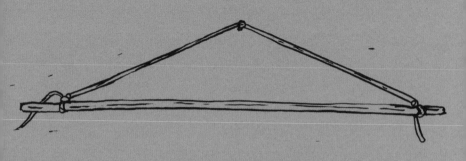

1. Taking one piece of your dowel and
one length of your shorter
pieces of cord, tie a Slip Knot
(see p. 16) at either end.

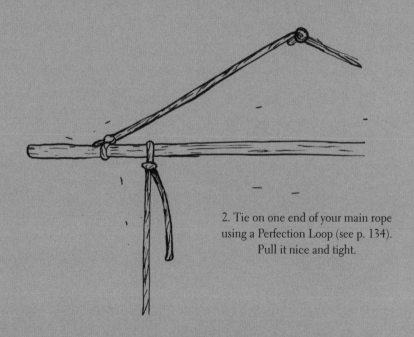

2. Tie on one end of your main rope
using a Perfection Loop (see p. 134).
Pull it nice and tight.

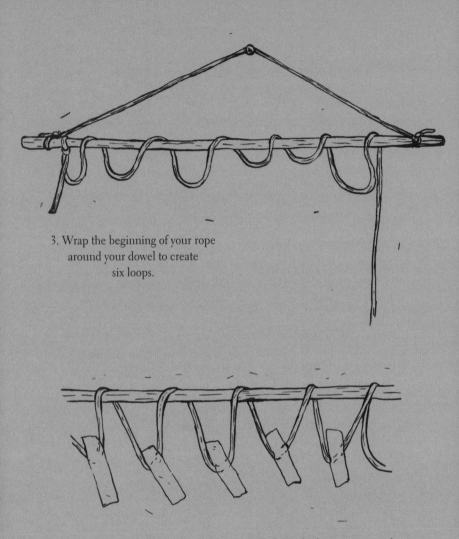

3. Wrap the beginning of your rope
   around your dowel to create
   six loops.

4. To keep the loops even, it is best to
   stick them to a surface using
   masking tape.

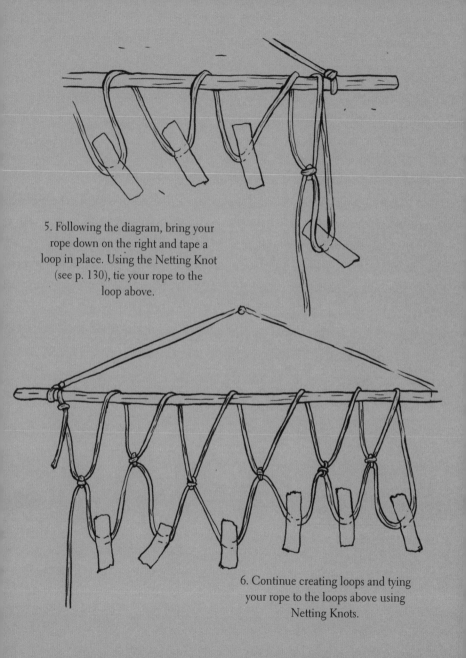

5. Following the diagram, bring your rope down on the right and tape a loop in place. Using the Netting Knot (see p. 130), tie your rope to the loop above.

6. Continue creating loops and tying your rope to the loops above using Netting Knots.

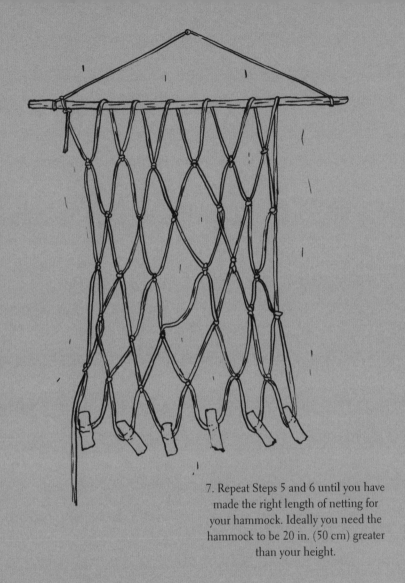

7. Repeat Steps 5 and 6 until you have made the right length of netting for your hammock. Ideally you need the hammock to be 20 in. (50 cm) greater than your height.

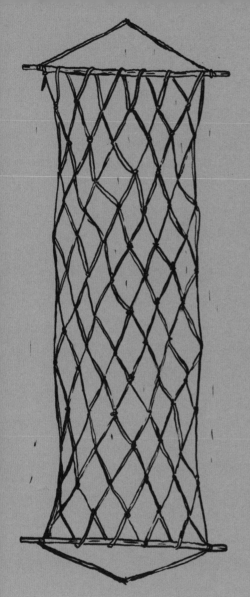

8. Once you have reached the desired length, thread your other piece of dowel through the end loops. Attach the remaining shorter piece of cord, again with a Slip Knot (see p. 16), and your hammock is ready to hang.

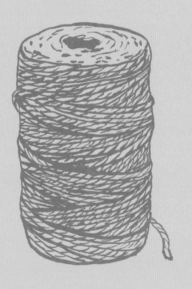

Sources

Many materials can be found around the house. Others, such as rope, can be purchased and should be of the highest quality possible. I have made sure that the materials used in this book are easy to source, either online or in local craft stores or specialty shops.

Rope

Most of the projects in this book have been illustrated using rope which is ⅛–¼ in. (3–5 mm) thick. You can use any thickness that you prefer; my personal favorite is a 4 mm natural rope. This is very easy to come by, especially online. The price of rope can vary depending on the thickness and length that you buy.

Websites
www.knotandrope.com
www.donaghys.com
www.homedepot.com

Wooden Rings, Beads, and Dowels

Any local hardware store should have a large stock of various thicknesses and lengths of dowels. You will need to decide what is best for the particular project that you working on. Rings and beads are easily sourced from craft websites, such as Michaels, or from your local craft supplies store. For the plant hanger (see p. 120) you could use leftover curtain rings.

Websites
www.michaels.com
www.joann.com

Scissors and Knives

When working on these projects I used the tools that I had around the house, but if you don't own any craft scissors you can easily pick them up at your local craft store.

Acknowledgments

I would like to thank the amazing team at Pavilion who were involved in putting this book together. Special thanks to Krissy Mallett for her endless support and guidance. I can't thank her enough for her patience and her ideas, even when we were considering a cat hammock.

Thank you to Maria Nilsson who illustrated the book so beautifully. It was a pure joy to see the book come together with her attention to detail and understanding of my instructions, especially the projects. Her level of detail is incredible, and the illustrations really do pull the whole book together.

Thanks also to Laurie who had to put up with the never-ending supply of rope littering the floor and who helped me when I got stuck when trying to find the right word.

Lastly, to my mother and father, who encourage me always to take on the biggest of projects, even when it doesn't seem possible.

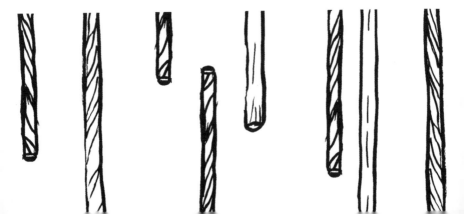